W9-AAW-385

Social Worker

Careers with Character

Social Worker

by Shirley Brinkerhoff

MASON CREST PUBLISHERS

Mason Crest Publishers Inc.
370 Reed Road
Broomall, Pennsylvania 19008
(866) MCP-BOOK (toll free)
www.masoncrest.com

13 12 11 10 09 08   10 9 8 7 6 5

Library of Congress Cataloging-in-Publication Data

Brinkerhoff, Shirley.
  Social worker / by Shirley Brinkerhoff.
      v. cm.—(Careers with character)
Includes bibliographical references and index.
Contents: Job requirements—Integrity and trustworthiness—Respect and compassion—Justice and fairness—Responsibility—Courage—Self-discipline and diligence—Citizenship—Career opportunities.
  ISBN   978-1-59084-324-6
              978-1-59084-327-7 (series)
  1. Social service—Vocational guidance—Juvenile literature. 2. Social workers—Juvenile literature. [1. Social service—Vocational guidance. 2. Social workers. 3. Vocational guidance.] I. Title. II. Series.
  HV10.5.B745 2003
  361.3'023—dc21
                                        2002154674

Design by Lori Holland.
Composition by Bytheway Publishing Services, Binghamton, New York.
Printed in the Hashemite Kingdom of Jordan.

Photo Credits:
Artville: p. 25
Corbis: p. 82, cover
Corel: pp. 34, 75
Dover, *Dictionary of American Portraits*: p. 6
Eyewire: pp. 31, 54
PhotoDisc: pp. 11, 20, 22, 28, 30, 35, 41, 46, 51, 52, 56, 57, 58, 59, 62, 64, 65, 67, 72, 78, 81, 83
PhotoSpin: pp. 4, 7, 24, 38, 40, 48, 50, 70, 73, 80
Viola Ruelke Gommer: p. 8

CONTENTS

We each leave a fingerprint on the world.
Our careers are the work we do in life.
Our characters are shaped by the choices
we make to do good.
When we combine careers with character,
we touch the world with power.

INTRODUCTION

by Dr. Cheryl Gholar

and Dr. Ernestine G. Riggs

In today's world, the awesome task of choosing or staying in a career has become more involved than one would ever have imagined in past decades. Whether the job market is robust or the demand for workers is sluggish, the need for top-performing employees with good character remains a priority on most employers' lists of "must have" or "must keep." When critical decisions are being made regarding a company or organization's growth or future, job performance and work ethic are often the determining factors as to who will remain employed and who will not.

How does one achieve success in one's career and in life? Victor Frankl, the Austrian psychologist, summarized the concept of success in the preface to his book *Man's Search for Meaning* as: "The unintended side-effect of one's personal dedication to a course greater than oneself." Achieving value by responding to life and careers from higher levels of knowing and being is a specific goal of teaching and learning in "Careers with Character." What constitutes success for us as individuals can be found deep within our belief system. Seeking, preparing, and attaining an excellent career that aligns with our personality is an outstanding goal. However, an excellent career augmented by exemplary character is a visible expression of the human need to bring meaning, purpose, and value to our work.

Career education informs us of employment opportunities, occupational outlooks, earnings, and preparation needed to perform certain

1

tasks. Character education provides insight into how a person of good character might choose to respond, initiate an action, or perform specific tasks in the presence of an ethical dilemma. "Careers with Character" combines the two and teaches students that careers are more than just jobs. Career development is incomplete without character development. What better way to explore careers and character than to make them a single package to be opened, examined, and reflected upon as a means of understanding the greater whole of who we are and what work can mean when one chooses to become an employee of character?

Character can be defined simply as "who you are even when no one else is around." Your character is revealed by your choices and actions. These bear your personal signature, validating the story of who you are. They are the fingerprints you leave behind on the people you meet and know; they are the ideas you bring into reality. Your choices tell the world what you truly believe.

Character, when viewed as a standard of excellence, reminds us to ask ourselves when choosing a career: "Why this particular career, for what purpose, and to what end?" The authors of "Careers with Character" knowledgeably and passionately, through their various vignettes, enable one to experience an inner journey that is both intellectual and moral. Students will find themselves, when confronting decisions in real life, more prepared, having had experiential learning opportunities through this series. The books, however, do not separate or negate the individual good from the academic skills or intellect needed to perform the required tasks that lead to productive career development and personal fulfillment.

Each book is replete with exemplary role models, practical strategies, instructional tools, and applications. In each volume, individuals of character work toward ethical leadership, learning how to respond appropriately to issues of not only right versus wrong, but issues of right versus right, understanding the possible benefits and consequences of their decisions. A wealth of examples is provided.

What is it about a career that moves our hearts and minds toward fulfilling a dream? It is our character. The truest approach to finding out who we are and what illuminates our lives is to look within. At the very heart of career development is good character. At the heart of good character is an individual who knows and loves the good, and seeks to share the good with others. By exploring careers and character together, we create internal and external environments that support and enhance each other, challenging students to lead conscious lives of personal quality and true richness every day.

Is there a difference between doing the right thing, and doing things right? Career questions ask, "What do you know about a specific career?" Character questions ask, "Now that you know about a specific career, what will you choose to do with what you know?" "How will you perform certain tasks and services for others, even when no one else is around?" "Will all individuals be given your best regardless of their socioeconomic background, physical condition, ethnicity, or religious beliefs?" Character questions often challenge the authenticity of what we say we believe and value in the workplace and in our personal lives.

Character and career questions together challenge us to pay attention to our lives and not fall asleep on the job. Career knowledge, self-knowledge, and ethical wisdom help us answer deeper questions about the meaning of work; they give us permission to transform our lives. Personal integrity is the price of admission.

The insight of one "ordinary" individual can make a difference in the world—if that one individual believes that character is an amazing gift to uncap knowledge and talents to empower the human community. Our world needs everyday heroes in the workplace—and "Careers with Character" challenges students to become those heroes.

Historically, social workers have worked to improve the worst areas of cities across North America.

1

JOB REQUIREMENTS

Social ideals are as old as the Bible.
As old as the commandment, "Love thy
neighbor as thyself."
—*Jane Addams*

In the 1880s, Chicago had a population of 1,099,850—and three quarters of those people had either been born in a foreign land, or were children of foreign-born parents. They often did not speak English or understand American ways.

When ***immigrants*** arrived in Chicago, which was called the "Gateway to Opportunity," they usually moved to a section of the city where other immigrants from their old country had settled. It was hard to learn new ways in a new country without knowing anyone who spoke your language. Settling in a neighborhood alongside many others who spoke the same language, ate many of the same foods, and had similar customs helped immigrants feel more at home. But in this way, the many neighborhoods of Chicago grew more and more separate, and soon began to function like small, foreign cities, all contained within one large American city.

During this era, the term "social work" did not exist. But many were looking for ways to help people in Chicago and other big cities, where labor conditions were dismal and even children frequently worked in ***sweatshops.***

Jane Addams founded the social work profession.

Jane Addams (1860–1935) grew up in Cedarville, a small village in northwestern Illinois. Her father was a prosperous businessman, and Jane received her degree from Rockford college in 1882. From the time she was very young, she was concerned for the poor in her neighborhood. During a visit to London in England, Jane was appalled at the poverty she saw, and though she had no idea of what she could do, she determined that she would someday do *something* to help other people. When she observed the social experimentation being done at Toynbee Hall in England, she decided to begin a similar center in Chicago, one where she could put her social principles into action and work for a better way of life for people there.

Jane's strong determination to help others led her to open Hull-House in Chicago's West Side slums. There she cared for homeless babies and girls in trouble, men out of work and lonely immigrant women who spoke no English. She trained assistants in what would now be recognized as social work; she lectured; she wrote books and articles; and she appeared before legislatures and governors requesting aid for the people to whom she was so committed.

Throughout history, people have helped each other. Help for the disabled was often considered charity. Help for the poor was usually given on an emergency, temporary basis, often by churches. But when Jane Addams opened Hull-House in 1889 and dedicated her life to helping the underprivileged people of Chicago learn to help themselves, her work became an ongoing model for others to follow. What she and her fellow workers accomplished there is considered the beginning of formal social work.

Many were inspired by Jane Addams' example, and similar projects were begun in other cities. But social work was not recognized as an occupation until after World War I. Following World War II, when thousands of people needed assistance to face the changed conditions of their lives, the need for social work grew even more.

Social work is a profession for people who have a desire to help others and make a difference. Today's social workers usually work in

Inspired by Jane Addams' example, social workers today work to help children and adults who live in poverty.

one of three categories: casework, group work, or community organization work.

- **Caseworkers** are involved in face-to-face contacts with individuals or families. This can include conferences in the caseworker's office, home visits, work with individual patients in hospitals, or work with children in schools, institutions, or homes.
- **Group workers** are usually involved in rehabilitation or recreation, or both. They may work in community centers, settlement houses, youth organizations, institutions for children or the elderly, hospitals, jails, or housing projects. Group workers may work with groups that have similar economic and cultural problems, such as migrant workers, or with groups who face similar disabilities, such as people with cancer. Social workers who deal with the welfare of people in public housing

Some social workers are employed in nursing homes.

developments are called *public housing community-relations-and-services advisors.* Those who conduct programs related to human relations or substance abuse are known as *human relations* or *drug and alcohol counselors.*

- **Community organization workers** analyze the problems of communities as a whole in an attempt to resolve them. For example, those who work with juvenile delinquents may find that the entire community must cooperate to solve this problem. Community workers are assigned to specific neighborhoods, to find and assist disadvantaged people.

Beyond these three basic divisions of social work, some social workers also teach in the nearly 100 recognized and ***accredited*** graduate schools of social work. A small number of social workers do research.

Social workers help people identify their problems and concerns, decide on effective solutions, and find reliable resources. In the process, they counsel their clients, arrange for services to help them, and often refer them to specialists who can help with debt counseling, childcare or elder care, alcohol or drug rehabilitation, and public assistance.

Within the three broad divisions above, there are many specializations of social work. Following is a list of areas in which social workers most often choose to specialize:

Professional ethics are at the core of social work. . . . Social workers' ethical behavior should result from their personal commitment to engage in ethical practice. The *NASW Code of Ethics* reflects the commitment of all social workers to uphold the profession's values and to act ethically. Principles and standards must be applied by individuals of good character who discern moral questions and, in good faith, seek to make reliable ethical judgments.

From the *Code of Ethics of the National Association of Social Workers.*

- **Clinical social workers**—offer psychotherapy or counseling and diagnostic services in public agencies, clinics, and private practice.
- **Child welfare or family services social workers**—counsel children and youths who have difficulty with social adjustment; advise families on care of disabled children; arrange for homemaker services during a parent's illness. Child welfare workers consult with parents, teachers, and counselors when a child has serious problems at school. They help identify underlying causes and develop treatment plans. Some arrange adoptions and help find foster homes for children who are neglected, abandoned, or abused.
- **Child or adult protective services social workers** investigate reports of abuse and neglect. If necessary, they intervene, and they may see that children are removed from homes and placed with a foster family or in an emergency shelter.
- **Mental health social workers** provide services for people with mental or emotional problems. This includes both individual and group therapy, crisis intervention, social rehabilitation, and training in the skills needed for everyday living.
- **Health care social workers** help patients and their families deal with illnesses, either chronic or terminal, and assist in handling problems that may get in the way of recovery or rehabilitation. They might start a support group for families of patients suffering from cancer, *AIDS*, or *Alzheimer's* disease. They counsel patients and family caregivers, and arrange at-home services for patients who will need assistance after leaving the hospital. Some health care social workers work as part of an *interdisciplinary* team that evaluates *geriatric* or organ transplant patients.
- **School social workers** consider and diagnose the problems of students. They counsel children in trouble, arrange for needed services, and help integrate disabled students in the school. They deal with problems such as student misbehavior or truancy, and advise teachers on how to do the same.

Criminal justice social workers do their job with prisoners and their families.

- **Criminal justice social workers** work with prison inmates and their families; they also make recommendations to courts. Probation and parole offices work with prisoners sentenced to parole or probation.
- **Occupational social workers** work in the personnel or health department of a corporation. They offer help to workers with emotional or family problems or substance abuse.
- **Gerontology social workers** help people who are older, especially those who cannot take care of themselves any longer. They may organize and run support groups for family caregivers, or they may advise family members about available housing and long-term care.
- **Social work administrators** work in management in hospitals and clinics.
- **Social work planners and policy-makers** research and analyze programs, policies, and regulations. They identify problems in society and suggest solutions, and they develop

Core Ethical Values as the Basis of Good Character

Why are ethical values important? Core ethical values, such as caring, honesty, fairness, responsibility, and respect for self and others, form the basis of good character. Our obligation to live by such values derives from the facts that:

- These values affirm our dignity as human beings.
- They promote the welfare and development of the individual.
- They serve the common good.
- They meet the classical ethical tests of:
  reversibility—(ask yourself, would you want to be treated this way?);
  universalizability—(ask, would you want all persons to act this way in a similar situation?).
- They define our rights and responsibilities in a democratic society.
- They transcend religious and cultural differences and express our common humanity.

Adapted from the Center for the 4th and 5th Rs.

programs to combat social problems such as poverty, violence, child abuse, homelessness, and substance abuse.

In order to enter the field of social work, a bachelor's degree is required. A B.S.W. (bachelor's degree in social work) is the most common entry-level degree, but some social workers major in psychology, sociology, or related fields. An advanced degree is now considered standard for many social work positions. An M.S.W. (master's degree in social work) is required for social work jobs in health and mental health and for clinical work certification. Social workers in public agencies may need a master's degree in social service policy or administration. Research appointments, and college and university teaching positions usually require a D.S.W. (doctorate in social work) or a Ph.D. In 1999, there were over 400 B.S.W. programs, 125 M.S.W. programs, and 63 D.S.W. programs or doctoral programs for Ph.D.s in the United States.

B.S.W. programs prepare students to be caseworkers or group workers. These are known as direct service positions. B.S.W. coursework includes instruction in social work practice, social welfare policy, human behavior, social research methods, social work values and ethics, and requires at least 400 hours of supervised field experience.

M.S.W. programs help students concentrate in their chosen field while continuing to develop their skills to manage large caseloads and perform clinical assessments. M.S.W.s' program includes 900 hours of supervised field instruction, usually called an internship.

Social workers must be licensed, certified, or registered, according to their state's professional requirements. Several credentials are possible for social workers, including voluntary credentials offered by the National Association of Social Workers (NASW), the Academy of Certified Social Workers (ACSW), the School Social Work Specialist (SSWS), the Qualified Clinical Social Worker (QCSW), and the advanced credential—the Diplomate in Clinical Social Work (DCSW). Some insurance providers require credentials before they will reimburse the social worker for services.

Full-time social workers usually work a 40-hour workweek, most of it in an office environment. However, additional evening and weekend work with clients may be necessary, as well as time spent handling emergencies or doing such things as attending community meetings. Some local travel may be required to see clients or

> ### What is Character?
>
> Good character consists of understanding, caring about, and acting upon core ethical values. . . . As people grow in their character, they will develop an increasingly refined understanding of the core values, a deeper commitment to living according to those values, and a stronger tendency to behave in accordance with those values.
>
> —the Center for the 4th and 5th Rs

Gerontology social workers help older people like this woman to live safe and rewarding lives.

attend meetings. While the work can be satisfying, it can also be emo-
tionally draining. Understaffing and large caseloads cause ongoing
pressure in many social work agencies.

Young people can prepare for a career in social work by taking a
college preparatory course toward a college degree in either social work
or the liberal arts. Required courses may include English, sociology,
psychology, human growth and development, and marriage and family
studies. Volunteer or paid jobs as a social work aide can be a good introduction to the field. High school students may apply to work summers as receptionists or file clerks at local social agencies, or as camp
counselors for inner-city or disabled children. A student may volunteer
to help in a retirement home one afternoon each week, reading to people who can no longer see to read, or may offer tutoring assistance in
public schools. Such work can help students decide if social work is the
career for them.

Even though social work has now become a recognized profession,
with all the areas of specialization described above, caring for another
person's good is still the foundation for this occupation. When Jane
Addams celebrated her first birthday at Hull-House, a friend sent her a
dozen roses. She took the roses to an invalid neighbor, a woman whose
family had come to America from Italy. The woman exclaimed over the
beauty of the flowers, amazed at their freshness after what she assumed
was a three-week journey from Italy.

"But these flowers are not from Italy. They grew right here in
Chicago," Jane told her.

The woman refused to believe her. "I've lived in Chicago for ten
years now and never seen flowers. They don't have flowers in America."

Jane realized that no American had ever taken the time to help this
woman learn what America was really like, or even to invite her to visit
areas of Chicago other than the slum where she lived. Jane determined
that she would be the one to help people such as this find a better life.

Jane Addams was known and recognized for her caring, giving way
of life. By the very nature of their work, social workers must constantly
interact with other people. It is in these interactions that strong, positive
character qualities are so essential.

These core character qualities are needed for social work (as well as for many other professions):

- integrity and trustworthiness
- respect and compassion
- justice and fairness
- responsibility
- courage
- self-discipline and diligence
- citizenship

In the chapters that follow we will look at ways each character quality is expressed within the field of social work.

Will you be satisfied with the fruit of your life's work? Will the efforts you are making now bring you satisfaction. . . ?

—Raymond L. Cox

College is a good time to sort out both career and character goals.

2

INTEGRITY AND
TRUSTWORTHINESS

*Sometimes, even the thoughts we
allow ourselves to think can
endanger our integrity.*

S elina had known she wanted to be a social worker ever since she
was eight years old, when she read a story about Jane Addams, the
founder of Hull-House. Later on, when other high school students were
talking to the school guidance counselor about possible careers and
struggling with what they wanted to do in life, Selina held steady to her
original goal. One afternoon each week, she volunteered to help resi-
dents at the local retirement home write letters or do crafts. During the
summer, she worked at the youth recreation program of the YMCA
downtown, because she knew these activities would help her understand people from different age and social groups. She saved all the
money she earned for her college years ahead.

By the time Selina finished her freshman year in college, she had
decided she wanted to work as a mental health social worker. She began
spending summers working as an aide at a state-run hospital close to
her home. While the experience was valuable, the pay was minimal.
During Selina's last years at college, her class schedule made it impos-
sible to hold a job, take classes, and complete her supervised fieldwork,

so she quit her job and concentrated on finishing her schooling, though her mounting student loans weighed heavily on her mind.

Selina's first position after college was at a large state hospital where some patients ranged from mild to severely mentally handicapped. Others were being treated for a wide variety of mental illnesses. Selina's days were spent working with her group of patients with mental handicaps. In team meetings with other professionals, including psychiatrists and occupational therapists, Selina helped assess her patients' progress and plan programs that would benefit them.

At last, Selina was doing the work she'd dreamed of for so long. She was helping people in the way she'd always wanted; she was truly making a difference. But she was caught off guard when she found herself struggling with an issue she never would have imagined would tempt her.

Selina's duties to her patients included doling out spending money to them each day. Unable to handle their money in large amounts, the patients had to depend on Selina to give them a small amount every

People with mental handicaps may have difficulty understanding the value of coins and bills.

The Question

Were the whole world good as you—not an atom better—
Were it just as pure and true,
Just as pure and true as you;
Just as strong in faith and works;
Just as free from crafty quirks;
All extortion, all deceit;
Schemes its neighbors to defeat;
Schemes its neighbors to defraud;
Schemes some culprit to applaud—
Would this world be better?

If the whole world followed you—followed to the letter—
Would it be a nobler world,
All deceit and falsehood hurled
From it altogether;
Malice, selfishness, and lust,
Banished from beneath the crust,
Covering human hearts from view—
Tell me, if it followed you,
Would the world be better?

From *The Book of Virtues*, edited by William J. Bennett.

morning. Some of her patients knew exactly how much they got and counted it eagerly. Some, like Joey, took the money with a huge smile, then looked at it with a slightly puzzled expression. Sometimes Joey gave his money away to other patients; sometimes he left it in the bathroom or the dining room and wandered away, never seeming to think of it again. When he did remember he had it, Joey usually bought several cans of cola and candy bars, then stuffed them into his pockets for after dinner.

"What a waste," Selina commented one day to the aide who worked with her. "Think what you and I could do with that money!"

Because people with mental handicaps are vulnerable members of our society, the professionals who work with them need to be people of integrity.

The aide, an older woman who had worked at the institution for years, looked at Selina with a surprised expression, and Selina said quickly, "I'm just kidding, of course."

But she found herself thinking how much Joey's $60 a month would help her tight budget. *He really shouldn't be allowed to waste all that money. I could just give him a smaller amount every day*, she thought, *and save the rest for him. I'd give it to him later, of course.*

. . . Of course, knowing Joey, he'd never realize if I didn't.

Selina felt a sudden sense of shock at what she'd been thinking, and she pushed the idea away.

Though she still gave each patient the full amount of spending money, Selina found herself watching Joey and a few of the other patients more closely when she handed them their money. To Joey, a shiny penny was as good as a quarter, and both were better than a dollar bill, because the paper money bored him. He liked to jingle and clink the change in his hands and pockets before he stuck it into the candy and soft drink machines.

And he struggles so much with his weight, Selina thought. It might actually be better for him if she limited the money he got each day. And she could really put that money to good use—not squander it on fat and carbohydrates the way he did.

Somehow, the idea no longer seemed quite so shocking to her. Over a period of several months, the thought of helping herself to Joey's money returned more and more often.

One morning, however, Selina found herself actually totaling up on a yellow sticky note the amount of money she could withhold from several patients like Joey. Just as she wrote the final "25" in the cents column, her supervisor looked in the doorway of her office.

"Morning, Selina! How's it going?" he asked. In one rapid motion, Selina ripped the sticky note from the pad and crumpled it in her fist.

"Fine!" she answered, then blurted out, "What did you want?"

Her supervisor looked at her oddly, his glance traveling from her startled face to the hand that clenched the yellow sticky note, then back. "I just wanted to say good morning, that's all." He shrugged and walked on down the hall.

Suddenly, Selina felt as though she were seeing the situation through different eyes. Her job had presented her with different options, but instead of evaluating those options from the perspective of honesty and integrity, perhaps even discussing them with a trusted advisor, she had been viewing them through her own self-interest.

She remembered clearly the first time she had considered withholding some of the clients' money for herself, and she could still feel the shock that thought had produced. But after she allowed herself

---

The four enemies of integrity:

- self-interest (The things we want . . . the things we might be tempted to lie, steal, or cheat to get.)
- self-protection (The things we don't want . . . the things we'd lie, steal, or cheat to avoid.)
- self-deception (When we refuse to see the situation clearly.)
- self-righteousness (When we think we're always right . . . an end-justifies-the-means attitude.)

Adapted from materials from the Josephson Institute of Ethics, 4640 Admiralty Way, Suite 1001, Marina del Rey, California 90292.

to think it several times, the shock had faded. Selina realized that by exposing herself to this thought over and over, she had gone through a kind of *desensitization* process.

Not only had she extinguished the guilt she felt at first, she had actually gone on to *rationalize* her course of action to herself by pretending that her motive—to apply the stolen money to her student loan—would somehow justify her stealing. Selina was astounded to see how far she had moved from her original commitment to integrity by desensitization and *rationalization*.

She pulled out her copy of the *Code of Ethics* from the National Association of Social Workers and turned to the section on integrity:

> Social workers behave in a trustworthy manner. Social workers are continually aware of the profession's mission, values, ethical principles, and ethical standards and practice in a manner consistent with them. Social workers act honestly and responsibly and promote ethi-

Trustworthy social workers have the opportunity to improve living conditions for children like these.

One key to being a person of character is to make ethical choices based on integrity.

Three Foundations for Ethical Decision-Making

1. Take into account the interests and well-being of everyone concerned. (Don't do something that will help you if it will hurt another.)
2. When a character value like integrity and trustworthiness is at stake, always make the decision that will support that value. (For example, tell the truth even though it may cost you some embarrassment.)
3. Where two character values conflict (for instance, when telling the truth might hurt another person), choose the course of action that will lead to the greatest good for everyone concerned. Be sure to seek all possible alternatives, however; don't opt for dishonesty simply as the easiest and least painful way out of a difficult situation.

Adapted from materials from the Josephson Institute of Ethics, 4640 Admiralty Way, Suite 1001, Marina del Rey, California 90292.

cal practices on the part of the organizations with which they are affiliated.

Selina knew she wanted to be a person of integrity; she also knew she didn't want to jeopardize her career as a trustworthy social worker. Selina began a new list, one which would help her stay accountable to others for her honesty and integrity. That evening, she would share with a trusted friend the struggle she'd just been through, and ask that friend to check up on her periodically to see if she was living up to her commitment to integrity. Here in the office, to avoid temptation she would make sure the aide was present when she gave money to the patients. She would also set up a spreadsheet showing the exact amount she gave to each patient and file a copy in the patient files, making it part of their permanent records. No matter how much effort it took, Selina knew regaining her integrity would be worth it.

Integrity is telling myself the truth. And honesty is telling the truth to other people.

—Spencer Johnson

Hospitals employ social workers to help patients and their families.

3

RESPECT AND COMPASSION

If you want to be a compassionate person,
then look for people who need your help.

A re you the person who finds foster care or group homes, or whatever they're called, for kids with handicaps?" The woman's voice
was harsh as she stared at Ken Neil from his doorway, as though daring
him to argue with her. "'Cause I'm at the end of my rope and my kid's
gonna have to go to one. It's been 17 years of her being in and out of the
hospital—in and out, over and over—one emergency after another, and
I'm the only one here to take care of it all, you hear me? And when I say
all, I mean *all*. The feeding tubes and the dirty diapers, getting her
dressed and undressed and cleaning up after her and—"

Ken, a hospital social worker who had had a very long day, sighed
and glanced at his office clock. Fifteen minutes before five was not the
time he would have chosen to take on a project like this, but he recognized all the symptoms of a burned-out caretaker.

He stood up and invited her in as though she were a welcome guest.
"I'm Ken Neil, and I'm glad to meet you. Won't you sit down so we can
talk?"

Disarmed by his courtesy, the woman stepped further into Ken's
office.

"Tell me about your daughter," Ken began.

The woman eyed him warily. "What?"

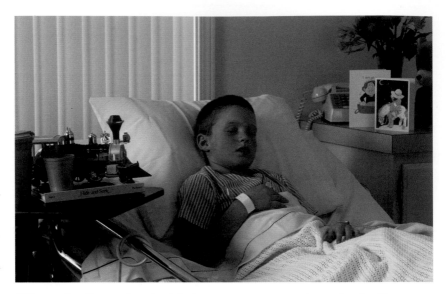

When a family member is sick, it can put stress on the entire family.

Ken repeated his request. The woman settled into a chair and began to talk, hesitantly at first, then more readily as she saw that he was really listening. Her daughter had been born with a condition requiring round-the-clock care. For many years, she and her husband had managed the care together, with frequent help from his mother and father. But in the past two years, both her husband's parents had died. Trouble was compounded when her husband decided he could no longer handle the stress and deserted them.

Social workers treat each person in a caring and respectful fashion, mindful of individual differences and cultural and ethnic diversity.
—from the NASW
Code of Ethics

"What kind of respite care are you getting?" Ken asked, when at last she finished.

The woman gave a snort. "You ever try to get that kind of help? I did, after my husband left us. There was so much red tape, I couldn't even get through the first form."

Ken knew there must be more to the story than she had told him. He let her talk on, trying not to notice that the clock was inching toward six. At last, he began to sense the real reason she hadn't been able to fill out the forms required to get help. Just to make sure he was on the right track, he pushed a list of respite care providers across the desk in front of her.

"Why don't you look this list over and let me know what you think?" he asked.

The woman folded the paper and put it in her purse. "I'll read it at home," she said.

Ken was nearly sure his suspicion was correct—she couldn't read. And he knew from experience that adults who can't read would rather do almost anything than admit it. He'd have to make this easy for her.

"Tell you what. Those forms can be awfully confusing. What if I go over them with you, step by step, and give you a hand. I really think, from what you've told me, that you're eligible for several hours of respite care every week and a home health aide as well."

Paperwork and forms can be confusing for many people. A social worker can lend a hand.

Deciding the "Who Counts" Dilemma

Who deserves our respect and compassion, and how do we decide?

In the laboratory at the National Institutes of Health, three monkeys have been used in experiments—including some that cause pain—involved in a research project on spinal cord injuries for over eight years. According to the director of the NIH, the next step planned in the research project will be to surgically remove the tops of the monkeys' skulls, insert electrodes to take brain measurements, and finally, to kill them.

Researchers would obviously never do to humans what they've done to these monkeys. But what is the basis for their decision? The message is clear, that in our consideration of who counts and who doesn't, we make judgments on the basis of who has *moral standing*.

An individual has moral standing in our opinion if we believe that how we treat him or her makes a difference, or that we ought to take that person's welfare into account for the person's own sake, not just for our benefit or the benefit of someone else. When a doctor cares for patients out of the belief that it would be morally wrong to mistreat them, and does not have in mind deriving benefits for herself, then her patients have moral standing for her.

On the other hand, a farmer who cares for his cows may also believe it would be morally wrong to mistreat them, but his motivation may be that mistreating them would diminish

Ken could see from the tears in her eyes that this news could make all the difference in her world.

"You really think I could get that much help?" she asked.

Ken nodded.

"I didn't really want to give my daughter up. I just couldn't figure out how to keep going. . ." She leaned her head into her hands and be-his family's income by decreasing the cows' milk supply. His concern is not for the cows themselves, but for his own benefit. The cows have no moral standing for the farmer.

Over the years, several theories have been developed as to who has moral standing:

- The anthropocentric (human-centered), and most ancient, view is that only humans have a moral standing, or that they are the only creatures whose well-being should be taken into account. The question as to which humans matter becomes even more complicated, however. For example, some views hold that any human creature that has the *potential* to reason, including a fetus, matters, and that both present and future generations of humans count. Other views hold that only a person who already reasons matter (therefore a fetus does not matter) and that only currently existing humans count.
- A view from the 18th century considers pain the fundamental evil. Therefore, anything that can suffer deserves moral standing. Under this view, which set the stage for the present-day animal rights movement, it is seen as immoral to inflict pain and suffering not only on humans, but on animals.
- A newer view, from the 20th century, claims that all life, even plant life, has rights to the protection of its interests.

What do you think?

Adapted from www.scu.edu/SCU/Center/Ethics.

gan to sob. Ken slipped out to his secretary's office to get the forms, giving her a moment of privacy.

Carmen was late to work for the third time that week, and her foreman was fit to be tied. Six-foot-two, he towered over her five-foot frame even on a good day, but now, as he leaned over her in red-faced fury,

Carmen felt she was facing a giant. "One more time and you're out of here!" he bellowed. "You got that?"

"Listen to me, please," Carmen pleaded. "I had an emergency—I—"

The foreman waved her words away with an angry gesture. "Lady, I have a production schedule to maintain here, and I'm gonna maintain it. *With* you or *without* you! Is that clear?"

"Please, just listen to me—"

Carmen watched the foreman stomp away, then looked around the factory floor in desperation, but the other workers kept their eyes fixed on the conveyor belts in front of them, scared to lose the rhythm of their work and fall behind. A feeling of desperation swept over her, and Carmen did something she would never have dared do before. Instead of taking her post in front of the conveyor belt, she turned and walked to the Human Services Office in the neighboring building. "I want to see the social worker, please," she said.

The occupational social worker listened carefully to Carmen's tale

All jobs have their share of tension; occupational social workers can help employees better cope with the stresses of their work.

Alcohol abuse devastates both individuals and their families.

of a husband who had recently returned to drinking after eight years sober. "Eight years he was a good husband! And we had everything all worked out—he finished his job at 7:00 A.M., drove home, and took over with the kids—we have four—and I'd leave for my job here.

"But last week, he got laid off. There was no warning. They just called all the workers together and announced that the plant was being moved to Mexico. My husband couldn't take it—that job was his life. He got drunk with the other guys on Friday night—" Carmen broke off to blow her nose and wipe away the tears streaming down her cheeks. "He promised me it wouldn't happen again, and I believed him. But when he came in drunk at 4:00 A.M. on Monday, I had to find a babysitter for the kids. That's why I was late—you can't call sitters at 4:00 A.M., you know? I waited till 6:30, and it still took me an hour to find somebody.

"He promised again that night he'd never do it again, but he did, and that day I drove the kids to my aunt's house, but it's an hour and a half away, so I was late again the next day. I can't lose this job, espe-

> ## Some Definitions
>
> **Respect** means showing high regard for others and treating them as you would want to be treated. Respect understands that all people have value as human beings.
>
> **Compassion** means we put ourselves in the other person's place. We feel that person's pain, and do what we can to relieve it.

cially now with him being laid off. But the foreman won't even listen to me. I've worked here for three years and never even been five minutes late before, and now he's threatening to fire me. . . ."

The social worker listened carefully as Carmen talked and cried, then shared with her what he could do. "If your husband is willing, there's a good chance we can get him into a short-term rehab program quickly. And I'll make some calls this morning and see if I can find a daycare center with room for your children. The company has some emergency funds that may help with that. I can also talk to your foreman and explain what's going on. And Carmen—" He pushed the tissue box closer to her edge of the desk. "—I really think you and I need to set up a time to talk every week. One of the things I do here is counsel people who are going through tough times, and I'd say that includes you right now. Would you like to do that?"

The social workers in this chapter were dealing with clients who had been shown little or no respect or compassion. Ask yourself:

- What makes us treat people without respect? Are we influenced by money, looks, or status?
- Who deserves our respect and compassion?

What do we live for if not to make life less difficult for
each other?

—George Eliot

School social workers work to promote justice and fairness for children.

4

JUSTICE AND FAIRNESS

*If we are people of character, we will be willing
to fight injustice wherever it occurs.*

Jonathan Parton was small for his ten years but quick on his feet. So it surprised Marion Clawson, the new school social worker, that he could be so clumsy. Today was the second time his teacher had sent Jonathan to the school nurse, and school had only been open for two weeks.

The first visit had been for burns on his hand. "I tripped and fell against the stove," Jonathan explained. "Mom was cooking dinner, and my little brother and I were kind of wrestling around in the kitchen." He smiled up at Marion and the nurse, and gave a little shrug. "Guess I learned my lesson about wrestling in the kitchen, huh?"

Today when the nurse brought Jonathan into her office, it was for a black eye in the making. The skin over his cheekbone and around the side of his eye was already purple and starting to swell. "Fell down the stairs," he said, and then squirmed a little under Marion's gaze. "Really. My little brother and I—we were wrestling upstairs, and we got too close to the top stair, and—" Jonathan broke off and shrugged again. "Mom says we're just too rough."

The nurse took care of Jonathan's eye, then came to Marion's office. "It's time to look into this more closely, Marion."

Marion looked at her, surprised. "What do you mean?"

"Jonathan may need help, and you're the school social worker."

"But he said the accidents were from wrestling with his brother—"

"They may be. And they may not. Marion, I've been seeing situations like this for years, and I have a bad feeling about this one. You have to follow up."

Marion thought of the child abuse cases she'd studied in college, but somehow, in this clean, upscale suburban community, such a thing seemed unimaginable. She held up a hand to stop the nurse from going any further. "Listen, I'll call his mother today, all right?"

Marion meant to call. She picked up the phone several times that day, but each time she started to dial the numbers, her stomach knotted up. What was she supposed to say to Mrs. Parton? She tried all day to think of how to start the conversation, but nothing sounded right. What if she said the wrong thing, and Mrs. Parton reported her to the school board? Or sued her?

I'll sleep on it and come up with something tomorrow, she thought.

The next day, the same thing happened. Instead of calling, Marion

Child abuse and neglect are all too common facts of life for many children.

All children have the right to be safe and loved.

decided to observe Jonathan in his classroom and on the playground. She spoke with his teacher, too, who told her only that Jonathan sometimes seemed a bit withdrawn.

By the time Jonathan's eye had healed, Marion was sure the nurse had overreacted. She continued to be sure of it right up until the fifth week of school, when Jonathan came to school with abrasions and purple bruising down the left side of his face. "Fell out of the top bunk," he told them. "My little brother usually sleeps up there, and I sleep on the bottom. But we switched, and, first thing I knew, I ended up on the floor." He winced as the nurse gently inspected his bruises. Marion went back to her office and tried to think what to do. Surely no one could have that many accidents in such a brief time. And yet, what if they *were* really accidents? She was still trying to decide what to do when the nurse appeared in the doorway.

"Marion, you never called, did you?"

Marion sat up straighter in her chair. "Now listen—" she began.

"No, *you* listen," the nurse interrupted. "We have a responsibility to

Child Abuse in the United States
(16 out of 1,000 children are abused.)

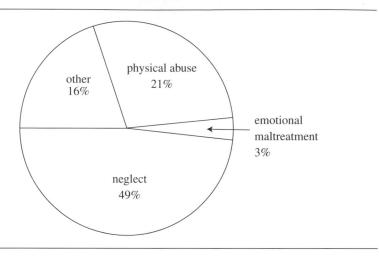

Source: Committee to Prevent Child Abuse, 1994.

this child, to make sure he is safe. I know you're new at this, and I know it's not easy, but it's your job!"

"And what if Jonathan and his brother *are* just rough? What if they really do just wrestle and get out of hand and—" She stopped. The school nurse was shaking her head back and forth.

"Marion, sometimes abused kids say what their parents tell them to say. They're afraid not to. There's no way to get at the truth except to investigate."

Later that morning, Marion made the call, her stomach in knots. Mrs. Parton seemed likeable, easy to talk to, even when Marion brought up the subject of Jonathan's mishaps. She answered all Marion's questions without sounding defensive, and even volunteered more information about other scrapes the boys had gotten into, but Marion was left with the uneasy feeling that she was missing something. In the afternoon, she spoke to Jonathan privately, but he repeated his story word for word.

The next morning, Jonathan came to school hugging one arm

against his side and seemed unable to move it. When the teacher sent him to the nurse, he kept telling everyone who would listen that he and his brother had been wrestling again. "Just roughhousing, like my mom calls it," he said. It seemed far more important to him that people believed his explanation than that he get treatment for his arm.

> Social workers challenge social injustice. Social workers pursue social change, particularly with and on behalf of vulnerable and oppressed individuals and groups of people. . .
> —NASW Code of Ethics

By the time the nurse examined Jonathan's arm and pronounced it broken, the boy was close to tears. "It can't be broken," he said quickly. "It can't. If it's broken, my mom will find out—please, *please* don't tell my mom."

Marion and the nurse spent the next two hours with Jonathan, try-

---

Moral Rights

HUMAN BEINGS HAVE THE RIGHT:

To be told the truth; to be informed about matters that affect their choices.

To do, believe, or say what they choose in their personal lives, but may not violate the rights of others.

To not be harmed or injured unless they freely and willingly choose to risk such injuries.

To have what has been promised by those with whom they have freely entered into agreement.

When deciding if an action is moral or immoral, ask: Does this action respect the moral rights of everyone involved? Actions that violate these rights are wrong.

Adapted from *Decision Making—Thinking Ethically: A Framework for Moral Decision Making*, by Manuel Velasquez, Claire Andre, Thomas Shanks, S.J., and Michael J. Meyer.

ing to calm him down, but he seemed scared beyond reason of his mother finding out. When they asked why she shouldn't know, Jonathan began to cry. "You called her yesterday," he finally choked out, "and look what happened. If you call her again—" The terror in his eyes unnerved Marion.

She got the principal, who agreed that child protective services must be called in. They sat with Jonathan at the hospital, reassuring him that he had the right to live in a place where he would not be harmed; that there were people who could protect him from his mother.

That afternoon, Jonathan, with a new white cast on his arm, was placed in a temporary foster home along with his brother. Months later, the court determined that Jonathan's mother had been abusing both Jonathan and his brother for years. Both children had learned to cover up what was really going on at home, and Jonathan had been quick to repeat at school whatever excuses their mother ordered him to give for his injuries.

Marion experienced weeks of remorse, knowing she'd let Jonathan down by not stepping in sooner. Whenever she saw him at school, she knew that if ever such a situation arose again, she would worry less about her own reputation, and more about her responsibility to confront the parent quickly.

Instead of holding back, she resolved to work through the following steps, then take action:

1. Get the facts from all involved parties.
2. Define the problem.
3. Decide on possible courses of action.
4. Ask:
    What benefits and what harms will each course of action produce?
    Which alternative leads to the best overall consequences?
    What moral rights do the involved parties have?
    Which course of action best respects those rights?
    Which alternative treats everyone equally, except where there is
        a morally justifiable reason not to do so?
    Which alternative advances the common good?
    Which one develops moral virtues?

If you are neutral in a situation of injustice, you have chosen the side of the oppressor.

—Desmond Tutu

Many social workers feel a responsibility to work with the homeless.

5

RESPONSIBILITY

*A sense of responsibility can
inspire us to act.*

C harles Loring Brace had studied to be a minister. But in the mid-
1800s, when he looked around New York City at the poor and
homeless children, the needy families in squalid slums, and the disabled boys and girls who had no place to turn for help, he decided that
there were other ways to "minister" to people besides standing behind a
pulpit on Sunday mornings.

Orphan *asylums* and *almshouses* were just about the only "social
services" for poor and homeless children in the United States then.
Brace decided he would take on the responsibility of giving New York
City another alternative.

Charles Loring Brace believed that having to live in an asylum or
almshouse could destroy children. He felt sure that meaningful work,
education, and a good family atmosphere could save the children from
a life of crime and turn them into productive, self-reliant members of
society.

Brace founded the Children's Aid Society in 1853, opened the first
industrial school for poor children, and established the first free school
lunch program in the United States. That same year, he also began the
Orphan Train Movement, which is recognized as the beginning of the

Thousands of children are homeless across North America.

foster care concept in America. Between 1853 and 1929, more than 150,000 abandoned, abused, and orphaned children from the slums and streets of New York City were sent by train to live with farm families across the United States.

> A good moral character is the first essential in a man, and the habits contracted at your age are generally indelible, and your conduct here may stamp your character through life. It is therefore highly important that you should endeavor not only to be learned but virtuous.
> —George Washington, in a letter to his nephew in 1790

Stuck in New York City with almost no hope of a successful future, these children, usually six to 18 years of age, were to be placed with morally upright farm families in the country. They were to be an extra pair of helping hands on the farm but were not to be regarded as indentured servants. The older children received payment for their work.

Brace's idea was unusual and controversial. The Orphan Trains went to more than 45 states, Canada, and Mexico. Some children found the adjustment to a new life difficult; others did fine. They lived normal lives, eventually raising families and pursuing careers. Though records are incomplete, the Orphan Train children who went on to the greatest success included two governors, one congressman, one sheriff, two district attorneys, three county commissioners, and many bankers, lawyers, doctors, journalists, ministers, teachers, and businessmen.

Back in New York City, the Children's Aid Society continued to expand its services. It opened lodging houses for both boys and girls;

The Good Samaritan

In the Christian New Testament, Jesus told this story about the individual's responsibility to care for a neighbor:

A man went from Jerusalem to Jericho. On the way robbers stripped him, beat him, and left him for dead. By chance, a priest was traveling along that road. When he saw the man, he went around him and continued on his way. Then a Levite came to that place. When he saw the man, he, too, went around him and continued on his way.

But a Samaritan, as he was traveling along, came across the man. When the Samaritan saw him, he felt sorry for the man, went to him, and cleaned and bandaged his wounds. Then he put him on his own animal, brought him to an inn, and took care of him. The next day the Samaritan took out two silver coins and gave them to the innkeeper. He told the innkeeper, "Take care of him. If you spend more than that, I'll pay you on my return trip."

Of these three men, who do you think was a neighbor to the man who was attacked by robbers?

[His listener replied,] "The one who was kind enough to help him."

Jesus told him, "Go and imitate his example!"

started the forerunner of the PTA; employed teams of nurses and doctors (with the help of the *New York Times*) to visit poor families, establishing a model for today's Visiting Nurses Services; began the "Fresh Air" program of providing summer vacations in the country for inner-city children (a program that continues to help children of the 21st century); opened free classes for children with mental retardation, free day schools for children with disabilities, and the first free school dental clinics in the United States. The list of other services established by this organization is literally too long to include. When Charles Loring Brace took on the responsibility of founding the Children's Aid Society, he transformed social services, first in New York City, and then across the entire nation, in many cases opening doors for social workers of the 20th and 21st centuries. His legacy has helped millions and millions of children find a better life. The Orphan Train Movement and other successful Children's Aid Society programs led to various child welfare reforms, including child labor laws, adoption and foster care services, health care, and nutrition and vocational training.

We connect hunger and starvation with other countries across the world—but in North America, thousands of children suffer from malnutrition and neglect.

Recycling is one way to be a responsible member of your community.

Ways to Be a Responsible Member of Your Community

1. Recycle.
2. Find out what your local homeless shelter or mission needs; organize a community drive to collect food, clothing, etc., to fill that need.
3. Volunteer to read to senior citizens at a local retirement center.
4. Volunteer to help senior citizens do crafts at a local retirement center.
5. Volunteer to teach senior citizens to use a computer.
6. Volunteer to walk a senior citizen's pet.
7. Plant trees.
8. Volunteer for a literacy program, to teach someone to read.
9. Help feed the hungry on holidays.
10. Volunteer for Meals On Wheels

Adapted from *The Kid's Guide to Service Projects: Over 500 Service Ideas for Young People Who Want to Make A Difference*, by Barbara A. Lewis.

Today, social workers continue to feel responsible for improving the lives of children.

Some Orphan Train riders are still alive. They keep in touch through the Orphan Train Heritage Society, on the World Wide Web, and through the Children's Aid Society. The Orphan Train Heritage Society is based in Fayetteville, Arkansas, and helps members both establish and maintain contact with their families, and retrace their roots.

All this happened because Charles Loring Brace felt he had a responsibility to help children in need. He could have ignored his sense of responsibility; it might have remained merely an uneasy feeling that tickled his conscious from time to time. Instead, he chose to act. His sense of responsibility became the springboard for concrete actions that changed our world for the better.

In your own life, are there things for which you feel responsible? Do you act on that feeling?

Goodness is the only investment that never fails.

—Henry David Thoreau

Social workers courageously stand up for the rights of children and adolescents.

6

COURAGE

*When we're not sure of the right course
of action, it's easy to allow fear
to influence us.*

S arah had never figured on needing courage to be a social worker. She had just wanted to help people. She'd pictured herself in a beige-toned, high-rise office, dispensing wise advice to clients who really wanted to hear what she had to say.

Instead, here she sat in a dingy back room of the police station, the block walls painted institutional green, listening to a story that might be true, and then again, might not. The 13-year-old across the table, Emma Ruggerio, had just told the police that she'd been sexually abused by her father, who also happened to be the head of Child Protective Services for their county.

That's when the police called in Sarah. As a Child Protective Services social worker, Sarah would be the one to sort out Emma's story and make decisions on how to proceed. It was up to her.

No matter how she shifted her position, she couldn't seem to hold Emma's gaze. Emma looked at her for only seconds at a time, then glanced away at the green block walls, at the floor, at the gray metal door. With her right hand, she twisted strands of her shoulder-length black hair around and around her thin forefinger. She answered questions haltingly, but Sarah couldn't determine if her reluctance was from

The relationship between parent and child should be based on trust rather than fear.

belligerence or fear—or if Emma might be concocting a tale to get back at her father for something.

Sarah had seen this scenario once before. A parent said "no" to something important to the child—and was suddenly accused of abuse. Some kids considered this the ultimate revenge. They had no idea of the consequences of such an accusation.

Sarah knew she had to report any such accusation of abuse and start the investigation process. She also knew if Emma was fabricating her story, she might take back her accusations and admit she was lying.

Sarah explained to the girl as gently as she could what it would mean to Emma's family if Social Services began an investigation. She tried to list the consequences in a matter-of-fact, straightforward way, for fear that anything more dramatic would frighten Emma so much she would back down on a truthful accusation. At the same time, Sarah wanted her to know that this could mean the end of her father's career,

Sometimes, a social worker may ask for the court's help in sorting out a damaging family situation.

Teenagers who face a harmful home situation may be resentful and withdrawn; a social worker needs courage to see past their anger to the root of the problem.

The primary mission of the social work profession is to enhance human well-being and help meet the basic human needs of all people, with particular attention to the needs and empowerment of people who are vulnerable, oppressed. . . .
—from the NASW Code of Ethics, Preamble

the destruction of his reputation and livelihood. Sarah had a fine line to walk—and she was scared she would take a wrong step.

When Sarah stopped talking, Emma stared at the metal door of the room for so long that Sarah worried she might never answer at all. At last, Emma's glance shifted to meet Sarah's, but only for a second.

"I know you don't believe me," she said. "But I can't take it anymore. Somebody has to help me."

Sarah still wasn't convinced. Emma had been through a thorough examination, and the doctors had found no physical evidence of sexual abuse. Yet statistics showed that false accusations were fairly rare.

Courage means you're willing to take a stand—all alone, if need be.

Sarah sighed. It would be so easy to disbelieve Emma. Because if she *did* believe her, that meant she had to confront Mr. Ruggerio . . . and she knew from experience that he could be a very intimidating man. How was she supposed to decide what to do?

What would you do in her place?

A Framework for Ethical Decision Making

- Recognize a moral issue.
  Ask yourself if there is something wrong, either personally or socially.
  Are there conflicts in place which could damage people, animals, institutions, or society?
- Go beyond concerns about legality.
  Does this issue affect the dignity and rights of individuals?
- Get the facts.
  Investigate the relevant facts.
  Decide which people have a stake in the outcome of this issue, and what that stake is.
  Determine your options for acting.
  Get the opinion of someone you respect about your list of options.
  Make sure you have consulted all persons and groups involved.
- Evaluate options from different moral perspectives.
  Which option will do the most good, while doing the least harm?
  Which option respects the rights and dignity of all stakeholders?
  Will each be treated fairly?
  Which option best promotes the common good?
  Which option encourages the development of the virtues and character traits we value?
- Make a decision.
  Considering all the questions above, which of the options is the right one?
  Get the opinion of someone you respect on the option you've chosen.

- Reflect afterward.
  Look back and determine how your decision turned out for everyone involved.
  Would you choose the same option if you had it to do over again?

Material adapted from the Markkula Center for Applied Ethics.

Character is indeed displayed in pressure-packed situations, but not merely so. For better or worse, every display of character contributes to character.

—Russell Gough

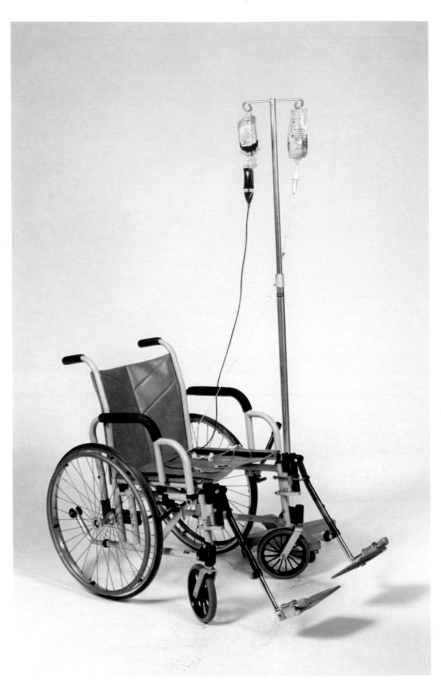

Social workers help elderly people find the resources they need to pay for wheelchairs and other medical equipment.

7

SELF-DISCIPLINE AND DILIGENCE

Self-discipline and diligence mean we do our
job well . . . even when it's not exciting.

Roger was starting to dread his once-a-week lunch with three other social workers. They'd all been in the school of social work at the university together, so their friendship dated back at least ten years now. Jana and Josh ended up working in child protective services, and every week they seemed to have yet another hair-raising tale to tell about rescuing kids from abusive adults. Steven Schmitt, who'd moved from Canada to attend the university, had ended up working as a criminal justice social worker. Though he sometimes talked wistfully about great social work opportunities in Canada, they could tell from listening to him how involved he was with his work with prison inmates and their families here in the States.

Roger waved good-bye when they dropped him off in front of the hospital, and sighed as they pulled away. He got into the elevator and pushed "9," the floor where he worked as a hospital social worker. In his mind, he went back over Jana's story about the four abused siblings her department had moved to foster care this past week. How he wished he could be involved in that kind of action!

Instead, he pushed open the double doors of his unit and found himself motioned into the lounge by three white-haired patients in wheelchairs.

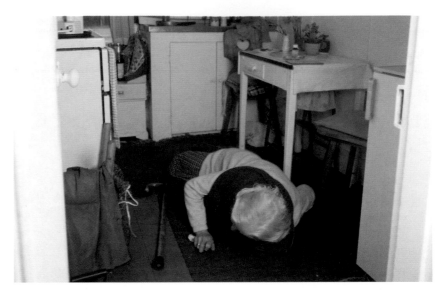

Elderly people living alone face many possible dangers, including falling; social workers can help them find ways to have safer lives.

"Mr. Davison, did you find out yet about the bed rails I need for when I go home?" asked Joan.

> In self-discipline one makes a "disciple" of oneself. One is one's own teacher, trainer, coach, and "disciplinarian." . . . There is much unhappiness and personal distress in the world because of failures to control tempers, appetites, passions, and impulses.
>
> From *The Book of Virtues* by William J. Bennett.

"And what about that electric wheelchair? Will Blue Cross pay or not?" Ramona asked.

"I'm being discharged after dinner," William told him. "And I still haven't heard from you whether or not the insurance company's going to pay for that home health aide you told me about. How will I manage if they don't? I can't even get a shower by myself."

Roger reassured all three patients that he was working hard to solve their problems, and he took at least a little satisfaction from seeing the worry drain out of their faces. "I promised you all that I'd do everything I could to get you what you need, and I haven't forgotten that promise."

He went back to his office and pulled up his chair to a desk nearly covered with paperwork and insurance forms. Sometimes, dealing with insurance companies nearly drove him to distraction. He had to have his wording for each diagnosis exactly right according to the insurance company's instructions, or his patients—the majority of whom had had procedures that would need extended recovery periods— might not get what they needed to function at home. Insurance com-

Character cannot be summoned at the moment of crisis if it has been squandered by many years of compromise and rationalization. The only testing ground for the heroic is the mundane. The only preparation for that one profound decision which can change a life is those hundreds of self-defining seemingly insignificant decisions made in private. Habit is the daily battleground of character.
—Senator Dan Coats

Social workers inform their clients of the assistance and insurance to which they are entitled.

Demosthenes lived in ancient Greece and was a contemporary of Aristotle. His great ambition was to become an orator (a skillful and powerful public speaker), but he had a speech problem and often stammered. Determined to overcome his problem, Demosthenes devised his own "treatment" by forcing himself to meet even greater problems.

First, he made himself speak clearly while holding pebbles in his mouth. He had to work so hard to enunciate in spite of the pebbles that, when he removed them, he found he had developed the ability to speak clearly.

Second, he trained his voice by reciting speeches and verses when out of breath, while he was running or climbing steep places.

Third, to force himself to study for two or three months at a time, he shaved half of his head so he would be too ashamed to go out in public and thus be distracted from his work.

You may not want to take Demosthenes' measures—but what are some ways in your own life you can build self-discipline and diligence?

panies were quick to turn down claims on a technicality. And then there were those treatment codes—with just a tiny slip of the pen, he could jot down a wrong code number, which could translate into weeks or months of delay in people receiving the care they needed.

Some social workers considered paperwork too much trouble; they spent less time and effort getting patients what they needed, but Roger had developed a painstaking system of checking and rechecking his work, just so he could avoid such delays. And his patients were grateful, he knew that.

But it doesn't measure up to rescuing four kids from abuse. Or helping the family of that man who got sent to prison for kidnapping.

Maybe, Roger thought, dreading his long afternoon of phone calls and paperwork, *I should have picked another area of social work—one with a lot more excitement and a lot less detail.*

Roger allowed himself the time it took him to drink a cup of coffee to indulge such thoughts; then he got back to work. He got clearance for William's home health aide just an hour before the patient was released. Roger couldn't help but smile at the relief on the elderly man's face.

"They told me not to worry," William said.

"Who told you?" Roger asked.

William pointed back down the hall with a hitchhiker thumb. "The other patients. They said not to

Principles of Professional Ethics

- Impartiality; objectivity
- Confidentiality
- Due diligence/duty of care
- Fidelity to professional responsibilities

Adapted from www.ethics.ubc.ca/

Elderly people have the right to safe, happy, and rewarding lives.

worry, because if anybody could do it, *you* could. And I thank you. I couldn't have managed without your help."

Okay, Roger thought as he shook William's frail hand. *So maybe it's not as exciting as some jobs. But I've learned to keep at it and I help a lot of people. And I care about that.*

That's what being self-disciplined and diligent is all about—learning to keep at a worthwhile job, even on the days when you long for excitement.

The noblest question in the world is, What good may I do in it?

—Benjamin Franklin

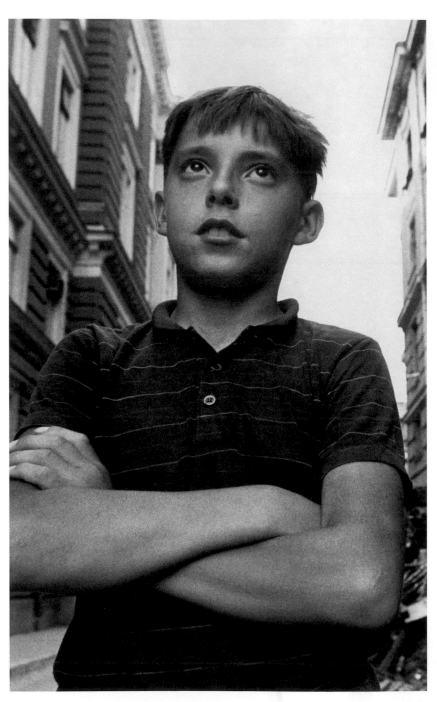

Father Flanagan worked for his community by helping boys like this one.

8

CITIZENSHIP

*Good citizens see the needs of others
in their country and try to find ways
to meet those needs.*

Today, a social worker is someone who has been trained for a particular sort of job. But in the early days of social work, a social worker was simply someone who wanted to help make the human community a better place. People of many different religions have traditionally shown this kind of good citizenship in the United States. Recognizing this, the government has recently begun the "Faith-Based Initiative," which would encourage even more aid from religious groups. Some of the great social work institutions of our nation have been founded by people of faith.

For instance, In 1917, 31-year-old Father Edward J. Flanagan was growing more and more disturbed by the orphans, rejected children, and young rebels the society around him didn't want. Backed by only his strong desire to make a difference, Father Flanagan opened a home in Omaha, Nebraska, for a handful of homeless boys. He managed to get $90 from a friend for his first month's expenses, but soon a steady stream of boys began arriving and the need for more money grew. Somehow, though, the boys were cared for, though the home didn't have all Father Flanagan could have wished. They had only sauerkraut for their first Christmas dinner, but boys kept on coming and the work continued to grow.

Eventually, Father Flanagan's home for boys would be called Boys Town (today, Girls and Boys Town) and would become known worldwide, with quality schools, athletic and musical training, and opportunities to participate in the unique self-government of the Village of Boys Town. Numerous programs have grown out of Father Flanagan's original dream, including the Boys Town National Research Hospital, a national diagnostic, treatment, and research hospital for children with hearing, speech, and language disorders; the Center for Abused Children with Disabilities (because statistics show that, while only 12 percent of all children are handicapped, between 25 to 60 percent of abused youngsters are handicapped); and the Boys Town Reading Center, which researches and implements programs to improve reading skills of "at-risk" adolescents. Boys Town also maintains a national hotline for troubled children and parents (1-800-448-3000), which receives between 300,000 and 500,000 calls every year. Father Flanagan's concern for neglected and orphaned children epitomizes the concept of good citizenship—and good social work.

Boys Town continues to help boys (and girls) across North America.

*Children who are neglected or abused are also more apt to have a
handicapping condition.*

The National Association of Social Workers expects its members to be good citizens, not only in their normal, daily work, but also if a disaster should occur. Section 6.03 of the NASW Code states: "Social workers should provide appropriate professional services in public emergencies, to the greatest extent possible." The Association takes this responsibility so seriously that they have issued a policy statement to give their members direction as to their conduct in the face of disasters. In the introduction, it states, among other things, that:

- of all the human health professions, social work is uniquely suited to work with and for people in disasters. Social workers can advocate for effective services and provide leadership in collaborations among institutions and organizations. The NASW urges that such disaster relief encompass the physical, developmental, psychological, emotional, social, cultural, and spiritual needs of those affected, in keeping with social work theory.
- people with the fewest resources, and vulnerable groups such as children, the elderly, and people with disabilities, are the most affected by disasters.

The NASW Policy Statement on Disasters supports for NASW members:

- effective preparation for disaster.
- enhancement of efficiency and responsiveness of disaster relief and recovery efforts.
- provision of mental health and social services to survivors.

- attention to the protracted recovery phase of disasters.
- attention to training, stress management, and support needs of disaster workers, in their position as victims and survivors.
- education of social workers and students in specialized knowledge and methods of trauma response and critical incident stress debriefing.
- development of rigorous disaster research, particularly intervention effectiveness research.
- the presence, commitment, and leadership of social workers in disaster services.

Adapted from the NASW Policy Statement on Disasters.

After an earthquake or other disaster, social workers step in to help.

Citizenship has been recognized as an important component of good character since the time of ancient Greece. The Athenian Oath, taken by young men in ancient Athens at the age of 17, stated:

We will never bring disgrace on this our City by an act of dishonesty or cowardice.

We will fight for the ideals and Sacred Things of the City both alone and with many.

We will revere and obey the City's laws, and will do our best to incite a like reverence and respect in those above us who are prone to annul them or set them at naught.

We will strive increasingly to quicken the public's sense of civic duty.

Thus in all these ways we will transmit this City, not only not less, but greater and more beautiful than it was transmitted to us.

From *The Book of Virtues* by William J. Bennett.

Civilization is first of all a moral thing. Without truth, respect for duty, love of neighbor, and virtue, everything is destroyed. The morality of a society is alone the basis of civilization.

—Henri Frederic Amiel

In North America's worst neighborhoods, social workers have the opportunity to do good.

9

CAREER OPPORTUNITIES

Opportunities to help others are
worth more than gold.

When Jane Addams opened Hull-House in Chicago, several men and women signed on to live at the house and help. They didn't expect their actions to change the world. They simply believed that "if one took the trouble to understand people, good might come."

The people of Chicago were more than generous at Christmastime to those at Hull-House. They sent baskets of food and gifts and candy—but just as that candy arrived, many of the young neighborhood girls, who had spent much time at Hull-House, suddenly stopped coming. Workers began investigating the girls' absence. They found that for six weeks prior to Christmas, the little girls had worked in a candy factory for 14 hours a day, six days each week. Most of them spent their day wrapping caramels in a hot, crowded room. The owner of the factory had used an old technique to guard against theft—he told the children to eat as much of the candy as they wanted, any time they wanted it. Hungry as most of them were, they devoured caramels until they became sick at the very sight of them. The candy that had been delivered to Hull-House by well-meaning people was from the very factory where the girls worked, and the sight of it made them sick.

The Hull-House workers investigated even further. They had known that some child labor existed in Chicago's neighborhoods,

Jane Addams worked for laws that would protect children like these.

Average earnings of social workers were $30,590 in 1998, with the top 10 percent earning $49,080 and the lowest 10 percent earning less than $19,250.

but they had never imagined how much. Child labor under poor conditions was affecting not only the children's education and social development, but even their health. Jane Addams eventually got involved in politics because of what she learned in this situation. Due to her efforts, Illinois passed its first child labor law in 1893. This was just one of the many good results of the social work done through Hull-House. The workers there took the time and trouble to understand the people they worked with, and much good came of it.

Social workers still take the time and trouble to understand and help people, and the need for this kind of work is expected to increase, especially in the following areas:

- Changes in our nation's ***demographics*** are creating a greater demand for health services. With better health care and nutrition, people live much longer than they did in other centuries, so more older people are in our population now than ever before. But older people often need more health care. As hospitals discharge patients earlier in order to control costs, more home health care will be needed, an area where social workers are being employed more and more frequently.
- The baby boom (the large number of births that occurred in this country after World War II) resulted in a large population group that is now in mid-life and continues to need social workers who help people deal with depression and mid-life career and personal issues. Social workers will continue to be needed in areas related to crime, juvenile delinquency, services for individuals with mental illness and mental retardation, AIDS patients, and families in crisis.

As the Baby Boomers get older, social workers will have opportunities for helping this group of people deal with the challenges of old age.

- Demand for social workers in private social service agencies and schools is also expected to grow. Schools will need to respond to rising teen pregnancy rates, the special needs of children from immigrant and single-parent families, and the continuing integration of disabled children into the general school population.

While social workers are required to meet certain training standards, academic knowledge alone is not sufficient. Character qualities are also essential. Social workers typically enter a client's life at a time of trouble, need, or crisis. It is then that a client most needs help from a worker who is trustworthy, compassionate, and fair; one who is responsible and courageous in his or her work, and who practices self-discipline and good citizenship toward all clients. Social workers with these qualities have the opportunity to do much good in their society, and to make a true difference in our world.

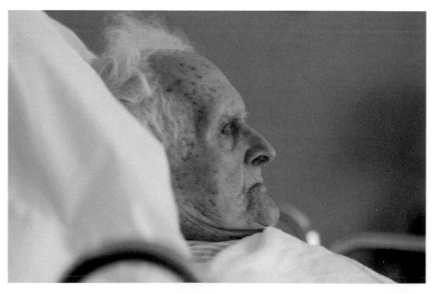

Social workers do what they can to help all those who are vulnerable and at risk for physical or emotional illness.

Medical Social Workers

Home health care services: $35,800
Offices and clinics of medical doctors: $33,700
Offices of other health care practitioners: $32,900
State government, except education and hospitals: $31,800
Hospitals: $31,500

Nonmedical Social Workers

Federal government: $45,300
Elementary/secondary schools: $34,100
Local government, except education and hospitals: $32,100
Hospitals: $31,300
State government, except education and hospitals: $30,800

Social workers have opportunities to reach out to everyone, regardless of age, gender, or race.

Like Jane Addams, some present-day social workers become involved with government as a way they can make the changes they see society needs. Alexa McDonough, the leader of Canada's New Democratic Party, earned a degree in social work and worked for Social Services before entering government. Although Ms. McDonough might no longer be considered a social worker, she is still working to make things better for her fellow citizens—and as a politician, she has the political power to bring about change in her society.

Let no one ever come to you without leaving better and happier.

—Mother Teresa

FOR FURTHER READING

Bennett, William J., ed. *The Book of Virtues*. New York: Simon & Schuster, 1993.

Hopke, William E., ed. *The Encyclopedia of Careers and Vocational Guidance*, Ninth Ed. Chicago: J. G. Ferguson Publishing, 1993.

Josephson, Michael S. and Wes Hanson, editors. *The Power of Character.* San Francisco: Jossey-Bass, 1998.

Judson, Clara Ingram. *City Neighbor, the Story of Jane Addams.* New York: Charles Scribner's Sons, 1991.

Kidder, Rushworth M. *How Good People Make Tough Choices.* New York: Simon & Schuster, 1995.

The U.S. Department of Labor. *Occupational Outlook Handbook, 2001.* Washington, D.C.: U.S. Government Printing Office, 2001.

FOR MORE INFORMATION

American Association of Marriage and Family Therapy
1133 15th Street, NW, Suite 300, Washington, D.C. 20005
www.aamft.org

American Association of State Social Work Boards
400 South Ridge Parkway, Suite B, Culpepper, Virginia 22701
www.aswb.org

Center for the 4th and 5th Rs
www.cortland.edu/c4n5rs

Character Education Network
www.charactered.net

Council on Social Work Education
1600 Duke Street, Alexandria, Virginia 22314-3421
www.cswe.org

Josephson Institute of Ethics
www.josephsoninstitute.org

National Association of Social Workers
750 First Street NE, Suite 700, Washington, D.C. 20002-4241
www.naswdc.org

National Board for Certified Counselors
3 Terrace Way Suite D, Greensboro, North Carolina 27403
www.nbcc.org

Publisher's Note:

The Web sites on this page were active at the time of publication. The publisher is not responsible for Web sites that have changed their address or discontinued operation since the date of publication. The publisher will review and update the Web sites upon each reprint.

GLOSSARY

Accredited Recognized as maintaining standards necessary for graduates to be admitted into higher or more specialized institutions of learning.

AIDS Acquired immunodeficiency syndrome, a disease of the human immune system transmitted by blood and bodily secretions.

Almshouses Privately financed homes for the poor.

Alzheimer's A degenerative disease of the central nervous system that causes mental deterioration.

Asylums Institutions for the relief or care of the destitute or afflicted.

Demographics The statistical characteristics of human populations (such as income, age, etc.).

Desensitization The process in which people extinguish an emotional response such as fear, anxiety, or guilt.

Geriatric A branch of medicine which deals with the problems of old age.

Immigrants People who have entered our country from another nation.

Interdisciplinary Involving two or more of the disciplines.

Rationalize To attribute one's actions to rational and creditable motives without analysis of true and especially unconscious motives.

Rationalization Defense mechanism in which the individual makes up complex, seemingly rational arguments to explain an anxiety-arousing or conflict-producing event.

Sweatshops Factories where people labor for long hours at very low wages in unhealthy conditions.

INDEX

BIOGRAPHIES

Shirley Brinkerhoff is a writer, editor, speaker, and musician. She graduated Summa Cum Laude from Cornerstone University with a Bachelor of Music degree, and from Western Michigan University with a Master of Music degree. She has published six young adult novels, scores of short stories and articles, and teaches at writers' conferences throughout the United States.

Cheryl Gholar is a Community and Economic Development Educator with the University of Illinois Extension. She has a Ph.D. in Educational Leadership and Policy Studies from Loyola University, and she has more than 20 years of experience with the Chicago Public Schools as a teacher, counselor, guidance coordinator, and administrator. Recognized for her expertise in the field of character education, Dr. Gholar assisted in developing the K–12 Character Education Curriculum for the Chicago Public Schools, and she is a five-year participant in the White House Conference on Character Building for a Democratic and Civil Society. The recipient of numerous awards, she is also the author of *Beyond Rhetoric and Rainbows: A Journey to the Place Where Learning Lives.*

Ernestine G. Riggs is an Assistant Professor at Loyola University Chicago and a Senior Program Consultant for the North Central Regional Educational Laboratory. She has a Ph.D. in Educational Leadership and Policy Studies from Loyola University, and she has been involved in the field of education for more than 35 years. An advocate of teaching the whole child, she is a frequent presenter at district and national conferences; she also serves as a consultant for several state boards of education. Dr. Riggs has received many citations, including an award from the United States Department of Defense Overseas Schools for Outstanding Elementary Teacher of America.